A CASE FOR

Serving

Also by THE Life@Work Co.™

A Case for Calling
A Case for Character
A Case for Skill

A CASE FOR
Serving

Discovering the Difference a Godly Man Makes in His Life at Work

DR. STEPHEN GRAVES & DR. THOMAS ADDINGTON

Cornerstone *Alliance*

FAYETTEVILLE, ARKANSAS 72702

Published by Cornerstone Alliance
Post Office Box 1928
Fayetteville, AR 72702

ISBN 1-890581-03-8

Cover design by Sean Womack of Cornerstone Alliance.

Printed in the United States of America

1 3 5 7 9 10 8 6 4 2

To our wives

Karen and Susan

*who have modeled serving
as a day-to-day way of life.*

Series Introduction

O ur offices are on the fourth floor of the second tallest building in northwest Arkansas. We have an extraordinary view of the rolling hills of Fayetteville from our panoramic picture windows. Although our city is growing, it still has the feel of a small town. Almost everyone knows almost everyone.

From that vantage point we enjoy watching cycles of life unfold around us. Unlike some parts of the country, we benefit from the whole assortment of seasons. The snowy mantle of winter melts into the sweaty heat of summer, with all variations in between.

We also watch the daily routine of hundreds of businesses. At the start of a day we can see the lights of other businesses coming on, like eyes popping open after a good night's sleep. At the end of a day we witness those same lights going out. The next morning it begins all over again. Then again. Then again.

We talk to many men for whom that description sums up their work experience. People come and go; accounts open and close. Creditors get paid; customers get billed. We pick up; we deliver. We punch in; we punch out. The workday begins, then ends. We earn our money; we spend our money. The cycle is unrelenting and unending. Then the cycle quits, and we die.

Is that all there is? Is routine drudgery what a man should expect from his work life and career?

What is the difference in the behavior and experience of a Christian man in his work compared to that of a non-Christian man?

What does it mean to be a Christian who practices dentistry? Does it mean that I have Bible verses on my business card? Do I share Christ with patients while they are under anesthesia? Or perhaps I ought to treat only Christian patients. If someone doesn't pay me, should I send their bill into collections, or should I forgive the debt and maybe pay for it myself? Should I work longer hours to display an incredible work ethic? Or maybe I need to work shorter hours so that I can spend more time with my family or serve on a church or community committee. Do I pay my employees more than the national average? Or do I pay them less so they can learn to live by faith?

What does it mean to be a Christian plumber? Do I cut my rates for Christian customers? Should I work on Sunday, or do I fail to respond to a crisis that comes on the Sabbath? Perhaps I need to hand out gospel tracts to other subcontractors on the job. Should I release one of my crew if he's incompetent? Or are Christians bound to keep every employee on the payroll for life? What does the Bible say about work?

A number of years ago we came across a verse in the New Testament book of Acts that serves as God's final epitaph for King David:

> When David had served God's purpose in his own generation, he fell asleep. (Acts 13:36)

Those words complete a description of David found way back in the Old Testament book of Psalms:

> He chose David his servant and took him from the sheep pens; from tending the sheep he brought him to be the shepherd of his people Jacob, of Israel his inheritance. And David shepherded them with integrity of heart; with skillful hands he led them. (Psalm 78:70-72)

David was a shepherd, a musician, a soldier, and a king. He had a very busy, full, and successful career. We would like to use those verses about David as the basis for exploring the making of a godly man in and through his work world. This short series will consist of four parts:

....David... *served God's purpose...*: A Case for Calling

He chose *David his servant...*: A Case for Serving

....David shepherded them

with *integrity of heart*: A Case for Character

....with *skillful hands* he led them: A Case for Skill

So, we are back to one of our questions from above. Is work basically an unending and unfulfilling cycle of activity? Answer: it depends. On what? On whether or not I know God.

According to King Solomon, one of the wisest and wealthiest men of all time:

A man can do nothing better than to eat and drink and find satisfaction in his work. This too, I see, is from the hand of God.... *To the man who pleases him, God gives wisdom, knowledge and happiness, but to the sinner he gives the task of gathering and storing up wealth to hand it over to the one who pleases God.* (Ecclesiastes 2:24-26; italics added)

Without God in my life, I might be driven, full of ambition, and very successful. I might even make it to the pinnacle of my profession. But I will not enjoy my work over time. It will not bring me fulfillment. I will be on a treadmill.

These books address a Christian man in the workplace. The definition and clarity that the Bible brings to a man and his work world are reserved for those who enjoy a personal relationship with Jesus. If you don't know Him, we strongly urge you to invite Him into your life. Then join us in exploring the topic of work in the incredibly rich, amazingly untapped pages of Scripture.

> May the favor of the Lord our God rest upon us;
> establish the work of our hands for us—
> yes, establish the work of our hands. (Psalm 90:17)

A word about our writing style. As coauthors, we speak in the first person when telling a story that relates to one of us as individuals. But we do not identify who belongs to which story. To help unravel that mystery, the following are some personal characteristics that will help sort us out.

Steve is an avid fisherman who baited hooks as a young boy on the Mississippi Gulf Coast. His appetite for learning and his energy for making friends have trademarked his twenty-three years of ministry and business.

Tom grew up in Hong Kong as the son of a medical missionary. He spent a number of years driving eighteen-wheelers, and he has taught at three universities.

We live in Fayetteville, Arkansas, love Scripture, and work together as business partners. Our companies and colleagues do work in organizational consulting and publishing. We have a passion to understand biblical principles that apply to work.

Book Introduction

Serving others.

It doesn't come naturally. We are born bent in the opposite direction. Instead of having a fine-tuned radar directed outward towards other people's needs and betterment, we are usually focused on taking care of ourselves. We are skilled at arranging information, opportunities, and even relationships around a self-interested grid. "What is in it for me?" is the single criteria.

Until we meet Jesus...the One who cast aside what was good for Him and acted upon what was good for us. He broke the grip that self-centeredness has on all of us. He taught serving to others. He modeled serving among others. He was...the Suffering Servant...for me...for all of us.

It still doesn't come naturally every time, but as a Christian I can learn and develop the art of selfless living.

This book will help establish what serving is, reveal what makes serving so difficult, and then portray a series of snapshots of serving being modeled.

Definition of Serving

The art of focusing
on someone else's interest
instead of my own.

"He chose David his servant and took him from the sheep pens....he brought him to be the shepherd of his people" (Psalm 78:70-71).

CONTENTS

Series Introduction   vii

Book Introduction   xiii

Definition of Serving   xv

1   What Serving Is   3

2   What Makes Serving So Difficult?   13
     The modern church movement
     The American spirit of independence
     Pass the ego biscuits, please
     Background and upbringing

3   What Serving Looks Like—Snapshots from the Bible   23
     The life and death of Jesus
     Jesus washing the disciples' feet
     The Good Samaritan

4   What Serving Looks Like—Snapshots from Life   37
     Serving your employees
     Serving your staff
     Serving your patients
     Serving your boss
     Serving peers and coworkers
     Serving clients

Conclusion   53

Where Do I Go from Here?   55

Notes   57

CHAPTER ONE

What Serving Is

The philosophy of "me first" has the power to blow our world to pieces, whether applied to marriage, business, or international politics. —James C. Dobson[1]

Albert Nobel left most of his fortune in a trust. Since 1901 the Nobel Foundation headquartered in Stockholm, Sweden, has been awarding annual prizes to those individuals who have marked our globe with an exceptional humanitarian effort.

Alfred Bernhard Nobel was born into a family of inventors and early entrepreneurs. His family had been manufacturing nitroglycerin when an explosion in 1864 killed five people, including Alfred's younger brother, Emil. Searching for a safer way to handle nitroglycerin, Nobel worked tirelessly until he concocted a way to pack the explosion into another material, which greatly reduced its volatility. In 1867, thirty-four-year-old Alfred Nobel patented and introduced dynamite to the world. Of his 355 patents, it would be his most famous and by far his most lucrative. The discovery of dynamite would become the funding backbone for Nobel Prizes. The average prize has grown from about $30,000 to about $825,000 in 1993. The list of recipients is an impressive parade of discoveries and advancements around the world.

- 1901—Jean H. Dunant (Switzerland), for his work at organizing the Geneva conventions of 1863 and 1864, which led to the establishment of the International Red Cross.

- 1906—Theodore Roosevelt (USA), for his mediation of the Russo-Japanese war and his intervention between Britain, France, and Germany concerning Morocco.

- 1952—Albert Schweitzer (France), for his efforts on behalf of the Brotherhood of Nations.

- 1964—Martin Luther King, Jr. (USA), for his efforts to bring about integration within the United States without violence.

- 1973—Henry A. Kissinger (USA), for his work in negotiating an end to the war in Vietnam.

- 1978—Menachem Begin (Israel), for his contribution to the two frame agreements on peace in the Middle East and on peace between Egypt and Israel, which were signed at Camp David on September 17, 1978.

- 1984—Bishop Desmond Tutu (South Africa), for his work against apartheid.

- 1986—Elie Wiesel (USA), for his books and lectures on his experiences as a survivor of the Nazi concentration camps of Auschwitz and Buchenwald.

- 1990—Mikhail Gorbachev (USSR), for helping to end the cold war and the Communist order in Eastern Europe, paving the way for German unification and democratic changes.

And these are but a selected few representing the Nobel Peace Prize. Every year since 1901, exceptional service towards mankind has been recognized and awarded.

However, the undeniable common thread woven through each and every recipient has been that none had the primary goal to win the Nobel Prize or to receive worldwide fame or a huge cash payment. Their motivation was to help, care for, and serve others, not themselves—pure and untarnished interest in other people.

Few Nobel Prize winners have intrigued the world like the small, frail servant from Calcutta, India. Mother Teresa won the Nobel Peace Prize in 1979 for her work among the destitute, the dying, and the orphan children in the slums of Calcutta. Read her address slowly, deliberately, and out loud. It tells nearly all that anyone needs to know about this model of servanthood.

Born: August 27, 1910, a Roman Catholic missionary

Address: Missionary of Charity, Nirmal, Hriday, Home for Dying Destitutes, 5A Lower Circular Road, Calcutta, India

The word *servant* is a rich, biblical concept that conveys the idea of working for and in the direction of someone else. There are well over a thousand references to servant, serving, and service in the sixty-six books of the Bible. It is a central component of the message of Christianity. It is a quality that God emphasizes and elevates as a universal language for all who have passed beneath the cross of Christ.

But what is serving at its core? When stripped to the basics, what does it mean and what does it look like? Serving is the art and act of focusing on someone else's interest, not my own. That definition will demand a role reversal for most of us in a country and a culture where self-driven, self-deserved attention is the common currency of exchange. Any Christian who serves others as a lifestyle might find himself in line for a Nobel Peace Prize. Actually, most of us will not receive a world-recognized trophy, but every act of serving will be registered with God and felt by someone.

Serving others requires a "Copernican revolution" of sorts. Prior to 1543, even the most brilliant minds had the universe framed around the wrong center point. Going against almost every shred of science, history, and experience, Copernicus placed not the earth but the sun at the center of the universe. This revolutionary idea eventually caused all the planets and celestial bodies to be reordered accordingly by astronomers.

Each individual must undergo a Copernican reordering to become a lifetime servant. We must redraw the universe around others, not ourselves. Joe White, at Kanukkuk Camps in Branson, Missouri, calls this the "I am third" philosophy. God is first, others are second, and I am always third. As an aside, the "I am third" award is the highest recognition passed out each week in the Kanukkuk sporting-camp system.

A national magazine front cover caught my eye the other day. At the bottom of the cover was a caption that read, "Self-Centered and Proud of It." The sketch that illustrated the lead article was a large, ever-expanding balloon head, loosely tied to a tiny man's shirt collar.

Serving is the exact opposite. It is the art and act of pumping someone else up, not myself.

In the last few years, an employee-evaluation tool has worked its way through the business community. It is called a "360-degree performance audit." Essentially it is the evaluating of someone's performance based on input and feedback from all areas that surround an employee. Those over us. Those under us. Those next to us. Those we buy from. Those we sell to. Suppose your company initiated a 360-degree servanthood audit? How would you fare? How would those around score you on being interested in other people, not just yourself? Would they say that you've discovered the Copernican revolution yet?

We live in a world that might periodically consider selflessness as a trait to be pursued. But the predominant message constantly piped in from our entire existence is, "What about me?" or "What's in it for me?" or "How about me?" When someone gets a promotion, we ask what that does to our salary. When a new strategic plan is rolled out by management, we are concerned about our workload. If the company had a bad year and earnings are down, we immediately grab a calculator and refigure our bonus.

J.B. Phillips had this to say about self-centeredness.

> Christ regarded the self loving, self regarding, self seeking spirit as the direct antithesis of real living. His two fundamental rules for life were that "love energy", instead of being turned in on itself should go out first to God, and then to other people.[1]

So is serving risky? Yes it is.

- It means getting to know people as people, not just human work machines.
- It means learning their names, their spouses, their parents, and maybe even their kids' ages and birthdays.
- It means getting involved with people, not always keeping a professional distance.
- It means becoming a good listener, not just a good talker.

- It means asking more questions and then really standing still, looking at them in the eyes, and listening to their response.
- It means remembering the conversations.
- It means taking the time to figure out how I can affirm someone else, get someone else promoted, get someone else's project funded, not just my own.

Regardless of my occupation, my title, or even my function, if I work around people, I can model serving. And get ready, because people hurt, people have emotions, people need direction, and people need leadership. And serving means focusing on someone else's interest, not my own. So how do we know if we are serving others? Robert Greenleaf in the book *On Becoming a Servant-Leader* takes a look from the other side of serving with these words:

Do those being served grow as persons: do they, while being served, become healthier, wiser, freer, more autonomous, more likely themselves to become servants? And what is the effect on the least privileged in society; will she or he benefit, or, at least, be not further deprived?[2]

Our business has grown every year since we started. The managing partner of our consulting firm likes to say we never have an opening, but we are always hiring. One of the joys of growing a business for us has been the prospect of building a long-term, high-performance team that is very business intensive and very ministry intensive.

The other day a new resume made its way to my in-box. The guy was impressive. Incredible credentials. Fantastic education. Unreal achievements. Off-the-chart life experiences. The more I read, the more I wondered what was not recorded on his resume. For example, where would anyone be able to detect a servant's heart and a servant's spirit? And then it hit me. What kind of resume would any of us have if the only virtues and entries we could include would be the achievements and accomplishments that others around us say we have helped them attain? If my resume was based upon my ability to serve others, how attractive would I be in the workplace?

Listen to these words from *The Message* that preview a job-focus sheet of sorts for Jesus, the Servant of all servants. "Whoever wants to be great must become a servant. Whoever wants to be first among you must be your slave. That is what the Son of Man has done: He came to serve, not to be

CHAPTER TWO

What Makes Serving So Difficult?

Without God, we cannot. Without us, God will not.
—Saint Augustine[1]

Some things come easily. Some come only through sweat, blood, and a set of worn-out, calloused knees. Other things seem never to come, regardless of what we do or how long we wait.

Some things are enthusiastically encouraged and fueled by our culture. Some things are allowed but not embraced. Other things collide with our culture and society like a salmon, fighting its way upstream to spawn, always against the current.

Serving others is not an easy discipline to develop, nor does our culture reward servanthood in everyday life. Yes, we pass out a prize or two a year to acknowledge huge and rare expressions of service to others. But usually we don't look for service to others to be valued in our community or to be a part of the script on television or the big screen.

Why is serving so difficult? A number of subtle pressures act as the river current to push us constantly downstream towards self-centeredness.

The modern church movement

For almost six years now, I've enjoyed a running conversation with a friend named Robert. He is the directional pastor of a very effective church in Little Rock, Arkansas.

Our discussion has centered around this question: What does it look like for a modern church to marry substance and innovation? Our initial conversation began when we both noticed a significant evolution taking place within the American modern church. Baby-boomer consumerism was alive and active in the membership rolls of the American church. The upside was that the church was still relevant. The downside was that the church had begun reengineering itself to become market driven toward its constituents, the customers. The structure began changing. Terminology began changing. Funding strategies changed. Staffing requirements and facilities changed. It seemed that any and every expression of ecclesiology was undergoing an overhaul.

So what is wrong with innovation and relevance? one might ask. Surely upgrades and face-lifts are permissible, even sometimes profitable. Yes, they are. Nothing about change is dangerous in itself. Actually, change can be a very good thing. But there were negative, unintended consequences that accompanied all of this modernization within the church. There was significant fallout.

Perhaps the most visible shift in the last two decades was the "felt-need" style of preaching that suddenly revamped most pulpits on Sundays and most homiletics classes on Monday. Suddenly any preacher who wanted to be effective and relevant started in his sermon preparation with the consumer in the pew and worked backwards to the Bible. Thus, many "growing churches" were offering a Sunday by Sunday dose of such sermons as "How to handle your money," "How to handle your emotions," and "Six steps to making your marriage successful."

What does this have to do with serving? you might ask. More than we might realize. Within the eclipse of a brief decade, many of the flagship churches in America had developed an additive level of self-interest. And it was being nourished from our pulpits. The expectation coming to church was now:

- What will I get from the message today?
- How will you help me with my problems?
- If I give dollars, what will I get back—a better building, a nicer nursery, a more professional choir leader—what's in it for me?

The good news was that unchurched Harry and Mary didn't know any better and they were at least being reached. The bad news was that we didn't convert Harry and Mary to *servant membership*; they converted us to *consumer membership*. We went from "What can I do to help you" to "I want it now, I want it cheap, and I want the best quality, and if I don't get what I want, I want my money back, now." Naturally it wasn't usually expressed this graphically, but the viewpoint was still predominantly "What's in it for me?" and not "What can I do to help you?"

The greatest consequence of this shift in the modern church is that many Christians suddenly had no checks and balances on their appetite toward self-involvement. If the church doesn't call us to give, not get, where will we ever receive that message? I'm glad to report that in the last two to three years there seems to be some correction taking place. As bitter as the pill might be, the church must always convert the culture, lest we be squeezed into its mold and be scored ineffective in our calling.

The American spirit of independence

No people have ever accomplished what we have in such a short period of time. We are the most self-contained, self-sufficient country in the world—or for that matter, the history of the world. Active in our bloodstream is a spirit of self-willed reliance that keeps America positioned as the lead goose, even in a flock of highly competitive birds. We can make it on our own just fine! We have since we cut the cord with the mother country, England, and we are certain we will always be the best. Just sit back and watch us.

Confidence—we have plenty for those who have none. But there is a downside to this strength. Robert Bellah, in *Habits of the Heart*, suggests that "[rugged individualism] might eventually isolate Americans one from another and thereby undermine the conditions of freedom."[2] Individualism, which in the past gave America strength, now threatens the survival of freedom itself.

At the core of individualism is the lack of accountability. The Bible, in contrast, calls us to be accountable to God and to other people. We are called to be, not rugged individualists, but members of community. We are to live in relationship to others.

To serve others effectively and to be served demand that we become interdependent. We have to become intentionally involved with other people. *Webster's Collegiate Dictionary* defines *involve* as "to engage as a participant; to occupy (as oneself) absorbingly; to relate closely; to connect; or to include." If I am to be a model of serving, I must become involved with other people. I must see it as my responsibility to help others, as well as allow others to help me.

Pass the ego biscuits, please

My kids acquired a guinea pig through an informal neighborhood negotiation between my wife and a friend's wife. Naturally, it was a done deal by the time I was asked to participate. Things have gone relatively smooth with the adoption. However, the cage is always dirty, the water bottle is always empty, and no one really ever has time to clean "Chumlee," much less visit with him. However, a recent discovery has revealed that our guinea pig has an uncontrollable appetite for carrots. The more carrots you feed him, the more carrots he wants. And the more carrots he eats, the less of the other food Chumlee desires.

The Bible clearly teaches that we all, somewhat like Chumlee, have a "flesh" that lurks about in the caves inside each of us. That "flesh" wants more and more and more when it is fed ego biscuits. Self-centeredness is part of the DNA of the flesh. The ability to arrange and order our environment to feed our self-interest is a natural instinct within every human being. Paul, the converted Saul, spoke a lot to those impulses that lie beneath the skin in man. In his epistles we are given the most detailed explanation of both "the new man in Christ" and "the old man of the flesh."

> Live freely, animated and motivated by God's Spirit. Then you won't feed the compulsions of selfishness. For there is a root of sinful self-interest in us that is at odds with a free spirit, just as the free spirit is incompatible with selfishness. These two ways of life are antithetical, so that you cannot live at times one way and at times another way according to how you feel on any given day. (Galatians 5:16-18, *The Message*)

Two questions surface regarding this flesh or the impulses of selfishness. First, does a Christian, after giving his life to Christ, still battle the flesh? And second, if we do still fight the appetites of the flesh, is it really possible to conquer sin's domination? The answer to both questions, according to the New Testament, is a double yes! Paul, in Romans 8:3-14, explained God's remedy for the limitations and sins of the flesh. God through Christ provided the Holy Spirit to believers. Now we have the real possibility of being controlled by the Spirit, not by the flesh. It is the Spirit whose life-giving power raised Jesus Christ from the dead. It is that same Spirit who can bring us life, help us grow, and give us the strength to quit feeding the flesh.

Background and upbringing

It is not automatic if you happen to be an only child, but a certain behavior pattern is called the "only child syndrome." Most of us have experienced at least one encounter with the "terrible twos" alive and well in the body of a thirty- or forty-year-old. No more diapers, no more pull-ups, but there is still a lot of mess that surrounds their people skills. This guy (let's call him Paul) actually believes the world revolves around himself. On the office wall in his mind there is a stretched map of all of the known universe. He is at the center (holding his "blankee" and bottle).

One day you meet the parents and family of Paul. All the pieces of the puzzle suddenly fall into place, and the cause of this dreadful self-centered worldview becomes clear. He was worshipped early and coddled well past the toddler years. Every time he was confronted and challenged, "Mommy made it OK," or "Daddy took care of it." He grew to become the lead part in a one-person, one-part play that ultimately becomes his program for the whole of life. This myopic, tunnel-vision kind of upbringing is difficult to shake. Some people's background makes it extremely difficult to serve others. They have no eyes to see and no ears to hear other people in the world but themselves.

CHAPTER THREE

What Serving Looks Like—
Snapshots from the Bible

There is the great man who makes every man feel small, but the really great man is the man who makes every man feel great. —G.K. Chesterton[1]

The last two sections of this book are examples of serving in action. There are snapshots selected from the life and teachings of Jesus, followed by six brief vignettes from the work world. These are not to stand as the comprehensive display of servanthood but rather to stand as selected illustrations to move us beyond analysis and theory towards application.

The life and death of Jesus

If you've gotten anything at all out of following Christ, if his love has made any difference in your life, if being in a community of the Spirit means anything to you, if you have a heart, if you *care*—then do me a favor: Agree with each other, love each other, be deep-spirited friends. Don't push your way to the front; don't sweet-talk your way to the top. Put yourself aside, and help others get ahead. Don't be obsessed with getting your own advantage. Forget yourselves long enough to lend a helping hand.

Think of yourselves the way Christ Jesus thought of himself. He had equal status with God but didn't think so much of himself that he had to cling to the advantages of that status no matter what. Not at all. When the time came, he set aside the privileges of deity and took on the status of a slave, became *human!* Having become human, he stayed human. It was an incredibly humbling process. He didn't claim special privileges. Instead, he lived a selfless, obedient life and then died a selfless, obedient death—and the worst kind of death at that: a crucifixion.

Because of that obedience, God lifted him high and honored him far beyond anyone or anything, ever, so that all created beings in heaven and on earth—even those long ago dead and buried—will bow in worship before this Jesus Christ, and call out in praise that he is the Master of all, to the glorious honor of God the Father. (Philippians 2:1-11, *The Message*)

No demonstration of other-person focus will ever be greater than what Jesus Christ did. Philippians 2:1-11 gives the full story, not selected sound bites. From this historic early church hymn lay some of the most clearheaded insights on serving to ever be found.

1. *Serving can be the lowest common denominator from which to build unity into any group.*

Few things are more powerful than a well-built, truly aligned team. One way to build commonality and consensus is to ask each team member to practice at least one rule. And that rule is: Focus on the other guy, not yourself. That can form the floor for like-mindedness, one spirit, and one purpose.

2. *Serving others will always adjust our perception of ourselves.*

Real other-person focus will eventually reveal parts of us we never knew existed. When I got married, a wise elder of mine in Fort Worth, Texas, said, "Son, when you're single, you think selfishness is a two-room shack. But when you get married, you discover it is a twenty-room mansion." In other words, genuine, deep relationship with someone else will reveal compartments and closets of self-interest that we never knew we were housekeeping.

3. *Serving must always be measured against the standard of the Suffering Servant, Jesus Christ.*

This hymn records the life and status of Jesus prior to His incarnation and then follows His life through crucifixion, resurrection, and ultimately exaltation. Here are four practical insights on serving that are woven into this biography of our Lord.

a. Don't clutch too tightly the things that "rightfully" belong to you (verse 6).

b. Take on the "perspective" of the one you are trying to serve (verse 7-8).

c. Be ready for your act of serving to be unnoticed, misunderstood, or even rejected (verse 8).

d. Know that the next world, not this one, is where the serving gets rewarded (verse 9-11).

Jesus washing the disciples' feet

Jesus knew that the Father had put him in complete charge of everything, that he came from God and was on his way back to God. So he got up from the supper table, set aside his robe, and put on an apron. Then he poured water into a basin and began to wash the feet of the disciples, drying them with his apron. When he got to Simon Peter, Peter said, "Master, *you* wash *my* feet?"

Jesus answered, "You don't understand now what I'm doing, but it will be clear enough to you later."

Peter persisted, "You're not going to wash my feet—ever!"

Jesus said, "If I don't wash you, you can't be part of what I'm doing."

"Master!" said Peter. "Not only my feet, then. Wash my hands! Wash my head!"

Jesus said, "If you've had a bath in the morning, you only need your feet washed now and you're clean from head to toe. My concern, you understand, is holiness, not hygiene. So now you're clean. But not every one of you." (He knew who was betraying him. That's why he said, "Not every one of you.") After he had finished washing their feet, he took his robe, put it back on, and went back to his place at the table.

Then he said, "Do you understand what I have done to you? You address me as 'Teacher' and 'Master,' and rightly so. That is what I am. So if I, the Master and Teacher, washed your feet, you must now wash each other's feet. I've laid down a pattern for you. What I've done, you do. I'm only pointing out the obvious. A servant is not ranked about his master; an employee doesn't give orders to the employer. If you understand what I'm telling you, act like it—and live a blessed life." (John 13:3-17, *The Message*)

Jesus was entering the last fifteen to twenty hours of His life on the earth. The unmistakable lesson of this story was that Jesus wanted to take His followers back to school for a refresher course in one single area. What was it? A quick scan of all of the Old Testament personalities? No. Was it a quick review of how to preach or how to perform miracles? No. It wasn't even a review of the theology of redemption. It was a brief but never-to-be-forgotten object lesson on serving.

Why serving? Because Jesus knew serving was the motivating energy that would allow the ministry of Christ to be effectively expanded when He was gone. There would be no book of Acts without it. The disciples would never look on a foot again without noticing the dirt and thinking of Jesus. Every dirty foot could become clean, but they would have to follow the Master's model. They would have to disrobe, be willing to get a little dirty, and wring out their need to be great in the basin of cleansing service. Some additional lessons from the foot-washing demonstration are:

1.   *A leader has to know what lessons are most critical to impart into his learners.*

Jesus was able to distinguish the major lessons from the minor lessons. If the leader cannot sort them correctly, there is a good chance the learner will confuse them. Servants must not confuse the strategic with the tactical, the temporal with the eternal, and thereby miss the greatest lessons connected with life.

2.   *Lessons that are modeled are the most effective style of persuasion.*

I'll never forget the first time I heard Professor Howard Hendricks say it. "More is caught than taught," he thundered from the front of the classroom. No questions. We knew it was true. Case closed.

3.   *Even the best students don't always connect all of the dots.*

Peter had listened, and Peter had watched. He clearly was privy to all of the before- and after-school sessions with Jesus. One could argue that no one had more of Jesus' time during the three-year school than Peter. Yet look at him here. He was still struggling to connect it all together. We should never grow discouraged or become impatient with those trying to learn the hard things of walking with Jesus. Serving others is certainly one of those hard things.

4.   *Every person can become a servant.*

Washing feet was a simple act that anyone who wanted to could perform. It didn't take strength of the arms; it took strength of the heart. It didn't take brilliance. It took humility. No age restriction, no education requirements, no special lineage, just a bowl of water, a towel, and someone willing to bend his knees to care for someone else's concerns.

5. *Every person needs serving.*

There were no clean feet in the days of Jesus. Everyone who was physically able walked the dirty streets and trails in open-sandaled feet.

6. *Know-how is not always the same thing as follow-through.*

Jesus emphasized over and over to His followers: Learn it fully, then practice it completely. Whether "it" is prayer, faith, or serving other people's interest, I have to translate my know-how into a clean set of feet on the guy next to me.

The Good Samaritan

The tale of the Good Samaritan needs to be framed for best application to be gained. The road to Jericho from Jerusalem was a twisting, turning, seventeen-mile road that dropped steeply into the Jordan Valley below. There were hundreds of hidden places along the way for thieves to hide. Robberies and assault on that road were not uncommon. Priests making the trip from the Holy City, Jerusalem, weren't uncommon either. What happened to the unfortunate traveler was not at all uncommon in that day. And to that setting, add the despised half-breed Samaritan who represented a genuine racial struggle during that time, and you can really understand the parable.

"And just how would you define 'neighbor'?"

Jesus answered by telling a story.

"There was once a man traveling from Jerusalem to Jericho. On the way he was attacked by robbers. They took his clothes, beat him up, and went off leaving him half-dead. Luckily, a priest was on his way down the same road, but when he saw him he angled across to the other side. Then a Levite religious man showed up; he also avoided the injured man.

"A Samaritan traveling the road came on him. When he saw the man's condition, his heart went out to him. He gave him first aid, disinfecting and bandaging his wounds. Then he lifted him on to his donkey, led him to an inn, and made him comfortable. In the morning he took out two silver coins and gave them to the innkeeper, saying, 'Take good care of him. If it costs any more, put it on my bill—I'll pay you on my way back.'

"What do you think? Which of the three became a neighbor to the man attacked by robbers?"

"The one who treated him kindly," the religion scholar responded.

Jesus said, "Go and do the same." (Luke 10:29-37, *The Message*)

So many lessons on serving can be connected with this story.

1. *People all around us are hurting and needy.*
    a. "Stripped" of self-confidence, of self-worth, of hope, of faith, of purity, of meaning, of opportunity.
    b. "Beaten" by competition, by failure, by pressure to perform.
    c. "Abandoned," lonely, gripped by fear and doubt.
    d. Left "half dead," helpless, and hopeless.

2. *We can avoid serving, even in the name of religion.*

Two religious professionals walked by the wounded neighbor. As a matter of fact, they even altered their course to "the other side" so as to eliminate contact and possible confrontation. Religious busyness often tramples right over human need.

Formalism, ritualism, and institutionalism can drive religious machinery right over hurting, needy people, all in the name of religion itself.

3. *Serving requires deliberate actions for any result to occur.*
   a. It takes initiative. The Samaritan took a relational chance. He knew he was hated and disliked, but he risked anyway.
   b. It takes adjustment. The Samaritan obviously was going somewhere himself. I doubt seriously his Franklin or Day-Timer had filled in for that day: Tuesday, May 15, 11:00 to 2:00, "Roam around road to Jericho looking for assault victims to help."

For years I thought the Samaritan was a full-time, two-donkey traveling medical unit. Not at all. He obviously missed his appointment and had his schedule wrecked that day. Effective serving sometimes results in that.

   c. It takes sacrifice. The Samaritan gave time. He gave money. He gave compassion. He obviously got his hands dirty helping to clean up the stripped, beaten man.

d. It takes sensitivity. The story clearly identifies the Samaritan as "seeing" or "spotting" the wounded man. Serving others always begins with being able to spot and recognize a person who could use a little help.

Early in this book we defined serving as the art and act of focusing on someone else's interest instead of my own. The Bible is full of stories that illustrate this life message. For example, David, Daniel, Nehemiah, and Joseph all evidenced early in their lives a servant's heart and a servant's actions. And undoubtedly, serving others was one of the predominant themes of the life of Jesus. It is impossible to read any significant section of Scripture and not see the strong serving theme in God's message to man.

CHAPTER FOUR

What Serving Looks Like— Snapshots from Life

A Christian man is a perfectly free lord of all, subject to none. A Christian man is a perfectly dutiful servant, subject to all. —Martin Luther[1]

(*Author's Note:* When we asked Christians to talk about how they serve others in the workplace, a dilemma developed. Because we picked people we knew had shown a passion for serving others, all were willing and eager to help. But the focus of their serving always has been on God, and none of them were eager to direct attention to themselves. The last thing any of us wanted was self-serving stories about serving. In looking for illustrations for this series, the topic was easily the most sensitive. So, while the content and examples in the following stories are accurate, the names of the people and their companies have been changed.)

Serving your employees

ANDREW COLSTON

Sometimes the most elemental of solutions are the ones that get overlooked in the high-speed culture of modern corporate America. Complex problems require complex solutions, don't they? If the question isn't simple, how simple can the answer be?

But when Andrew Colston approaches the daunting task of serving his employees, he begins with the most basic, and simplest, of foundations: prayer.

Andrew, the president and founder of a successful retail business, has around two hundred employees. And every morning before reporting to work, the man at the top of their corporate ladder gets down on his knees and prays for them.

Andrew, whose wife often joins him in prayer, asks God to bless his employees and make them happy and also productive in their work. If they are happy, Andrew knows they will be productive. If they are productive, Andrew knows they will be happy.

But Andrew also can be specific in his prayers. He isn't able to pray for every employee every day. But over the course of time, he works his way through the entire company—name by name, need by need. Then he starts over again.

The employees, of course, benefit from the prayers, even though most of them never know that their boss has lifted them up.

The process also prepares Andrew for his day at the office. He arrives not as a detached corporate executive who ascends to an isolated ivory tower but as a man who is sensitized to the needs of the people who work for him. He becomes challenged to find out more and more about each employee, which allows him to serve their complex needs in any number of simple ways—the first, of course, being prayer.

Andrew Colston's prayers aren't always answered the way he would like. And the ones that are answered aren't always answered on his timetable.

But Paul Lee, for one, is grateful that Andrew never let such frustrations stop him from modeling the Christian life.

Paul has worked for Andrew for more than twenty-six years, but it was only recently that he came to know Christ. For years, Andrew has patiently modeled the gospel in the workplace, hoping and praying that it would have an impact on people such as Paul. In time, it did. Andrew doesn't try to convert anyone by force, which is one of the things Paul appreciates most about his boss. Paul wasn't won over through "gorilla evangelism," but because each day he sees leadership by example. He sees a man who always is available, a man who listens, and a man who cares. He sees a man who looks for solutions without placing blame, a man who always sees more in other people than those people see in themselves. He sees a man who leads with his heart and his soul, not with selfish impulses. And he sees a man who is rewarded for his lifestyle.

Through the years, Andrew's leadership has produced a company that is known as much for its integrity as its profitability. And in the process, he has served as a personal beam of light that eventually has led many around him, like Paul, out of the darkness.

Stan Morris

When the National Collegiate Athletic Association's main office in Kansas City was at its bureaucratic worst, employees were considered tardy if they arrived after 8:30 a.m.

Their thermal drapes had to be pulled, their desks had to be cleared at the end of each day, and no day would end prior to 5 p.m. Every employee worked every other Saturday and adhered to a strict dress code. And no one took a coffee break or was allowed to even bring a drink of any sort to their desk.

There was even a manual—NCAA Office Policies and Procedures—that was more than a hundred pages of rules for the workplace.

It was, one would imagine, about as opposite as any business could be run from the small but profitable company Stan Morris's family has operated for three generations.

Stan has his own dress code: Everyone has to come to work dressed. He has rules about the hours his thirteen employees keep: Be here when you are supposed to be here unless you need to be somewhere else. And the only clock his employees punch is the one that wakes them up each morning.

Stan believes he best serves his employees by treating them like family. That doesn't mean they sleep at his house, eat his food, and ask his wife to wash their laundry. But it does mean they can expect a certain leeway when a request is legitimate (and maybe an occasional cookout).

All Stan asks for in return is that they treat him and his company the same way—like it is part of their family.

Stan realizes this approach is only as good as the people he hires. But, so far, it has worked to the betterment of everyone involved.

Members of Stan's support staff are allowed to take off if their kids have doctor's appointments or school functions. But they willingly come in early or work through their lunch hour to make up the time. And because Stan serves them by providing flexible hours—a privilege they would like to keep—they serve each other by picking up the slack for anyone who needs it.

There have been those who abuse the system, of course. But Stan sees the silver lining there, as well. Take, for instance, the man he hired who spent most of his days in the back room working his own multilevel market interest. Stan was aware of the problem, but, as usual, he was willing to give the guy a second chance. So he headed to the back room to suggest that the employee spend less time making personal calls and more time representing the person who was providing the office and the company car.

But before he could get the words out of his mouth, the man announced that he had been offered a coaching job in a neighboring state and that he planned to accept the position.

The way Stan sees it, God took care of the problem. And even though the man had cost the company money, Stan felt blessed by the opportunity to see God's hand work in the situation. It was an opportunity that might never have come if he had been following some hundred-page manual.

Serving your staff

JIM ALLEN

Jim Allen's vocation is all about serving others, but this pastor of a growing Bible church realizes there is a tendency to overlook the people who are paid to serve him.

It is a common pitfall for busy bosses. They are eager to serve their clients, customers, or, in this case, parishioners, but in doing so, they ignore the needs of their hardworking staff. They become blinded to the needs of the people they are in the best position to serve.

Jim tries to avoid this pitfall by practicing what he calls "water-fountain management." It is his mechanism for building relationships with the people who work in his church. Jim spends as much time as possible visiting with the people on his staff, learning their strengths and weaknesses, their hopes and their dreams, their problems and their victories.

Jim can be an extremely task-focused individual, and there are times when that is an extremely important aspect of his job. But for brief stretches of time each day, he turns off that side of his personality and turns on the relationship-focused side.

He visits the water fountain.

The knowledge Jim drinks in from around "the water fountain" helps him know and serve the needs of his staff. If he knows a person's strengths, he can hold that person accountable so that those strengths don't grow out of control. If he knows a person's weaknesses, he can offer encouragement or practical advice to help build them up.

If he knows their needs, he is more likely to meet their needs.

That is why he offered a hand to the building superintendent when it came time to lift a new wall for an addition to the church office. Jim didn't wait to find out about the man's back problem by hearing a scream of agony from a guy with a wrenched muscle. Instead, he already knew the man didn't need to do any heavy lifting. He had learned that information weeks earlier during one of their regular chats; then Jim had stored the information away. Now he was there to serve this staff member in a very practical way. In doing so, Jim lifted not only the wall but also the man standing beside him.

Serving your patients

CLIFF IVERS

Cliff Ivers doesn't like going to the dentist, which is one of the big reasons why he is such a patient-friendly dentist himself.

Cliff tries to operate his practice by adhering to a modified version of the Golden Rule: Treat your patients the way you would want to be treated if you were the patient. It is a philosophy that works particularly well for a man who would much rather be standing beside the chair than sitting in it.

When his patients sit down, Cliff wants them to know that he has been there before, that he knows what it is like, and that he will do everything within his power to make the experience as pleasant as possible.

He keeps a twinkle in his eyes, a smile on his face, and good humor in his voice, even on the days when he feels his worst.

But Cliff's style requires more than a comforting chair-side manner.

Cliff tries to view his entire work world through the patient's eyes. What do they see when they come through the door? How does everything from the wallpaper to the magazines to the staff work to affect the patient's mood? All of these things are important parts of Cliff's goal of serving his patients.

He doesn't want his practice to become assembly-line dentistry with a "drill 'em, fill 'em, and bill 'em" mentality. He's committed to something much more personal, and that commitment extends to every aspect of his office.

Cliff makes a deliberate attempt to create an office style and culture around him that is friendly to his patients. That means he has to be upbeat and encouraging. And that means he has to find ways to reward his staff for following suit. It means spending a little extra on incentive programs for his staff. It means reinvesting profits back into people and systems. Recently, Cliff bought a new piece of equipment that costs more than either of his automobiles. He thought he would never get over the sticker shock. And it means spending a little extra to keep the office decor fresh and up-to-date.

In short, it means doing whatever it takes to satisfy and serve the most cranky patient Cliff could encounter—himself.

Serving your boss

TED MELVIN

If Ted Melvin's boss can order from a menu, then the senior executive of a Fortune 25 company should survive just fine.

As the director of purchasing and one of eight direct reports to one of the company's senior executives, Ted wants to carry out his duties so that his boss has only two major concerns—what to eat and what to drink. Everything else he can leave to Ted.

It is an approach Ted has taken from the biblical life of Joseph. The Old Testament says Joseph served Potiphar to such a degree that all Potiphar had to worry about was what he would eat and what he would drink. Everything else he put in Joseph's charge; Potiphar did not concern himself with it anymore.

The simple principle is the driving force behind Ted's philosophy of servanthood in the workplace. He never wants his boss to worry about anything that Ted is in charge of carrying out. When Ted is given an assignment, he doesn't want his boss to think about it again until complete and competent results have been delivered—ahead of schedule.

This philosophy serves Ted's boss well because it allows him to focus on other issues. It serves Ted well in a spiritual sense because it is biblically sound, and it serves him well in a secular sense because it earns him the respect and admiration of his boss. And since he models the philosophy well for the people who report to him, it serves others well. It touches people above, below, and all around him.

Ted proves his value to his boss again and again. And Ted's charges learn to show their value to Ted again and again. In turn, everyone in the loop becomes valuable to the organization. And when their work is done, all they need to think about is what to eat and what to drink.

Serving peers and coworkers

EDWARD MARVIN

Keeping a watchful eye on his fellow pilots had become second nature for Edward, just as it had become second nature for his fellow pilots to keep an eye on him.

They all knew the demands of their job as pilots for an international missionary ministry, and an instinctive bond had developed between the members of the team. They were there to take care of each other, to make each other better, and to keep the entire crew flying with maximum productivity. The result was that each of the individual parts became stronger than it ever could be alone.

That is why Edward hardly gave a second thought to the idea of flying every day for three straight weeks so that the pilots who needed a rest could get it. He just did it. And that is why the pilots who needed a break hardly gave a second thought to allowing Edward to take some of their flights.

They would do, and often did, the exact same thing for him. It was that way for Edward's twelve years as a pilot for this ministry, and it was that way during his yearlong stint as an aviator during Vietnam.

The culture of serving one's peers was intentionally cultivated and grown by these men until its roots dug deep into their very souls. And it is a culture Edward has carried with him into the corporate world at every stop in his career.

To Edward, serving a fellow airman by taking one of his flights is no different than spending time with a new employee to make sure his adjustment to the job goes smoothly. That person eventually would become acclimated to the new environment, just as the other pilots would make their scheduled trips even if they were tired.

But in both cases, the whole process went more smoothly with a little extra effort—effort that was unsolicited and unrewarded in secular terms—from someone willing to serve.

It is a type of spiritually based leadership, one that follows the example set by Jesus and one that others often adopt and spread to those around them until pretty soon no one is really sure who is leading this call to servanthood. But they all know they are better off because it is there.

Serving clients

TIM DAILEY

The family business began back in 1879, and sometime during the second generation's proprietorship, a company motto was established.

It was a simple four-word credo: Service beyond the contract.

It sounded good, and Tim, the third-generation owner and president, has no reason to believe there was anything cosmetic about the stance his father had proclaimed for the business. But since his father, like his grandfather, wasn't a Christian, Tim knows the attraction to a biblically supported philosophy was purely coincidental.

For Tim, however, the motto is much more than something he stamps on his stationery or pastes in bold letters across the company's ad in the yellow pages. It is a way of life.

Tim sees it as part of his Christian obligation to live out that motto of service to his customers, even if it isn't always the most profitable avenue to take.

As president of an independent insurance agency, Tim knows he is in an industry that often pays lip service to such flashy mottoes.

Not Tim.

Whenever a customer's policy is due for renewal, Tim always includes a personal letter that outlines the coverage the policyholder has and the options available for the renewal. Many times, these options lower both the premium for the customer and the commission for Tim's agency.

When a car reaches the age where comprehensive and collision coverages no longer are cost-effective, Tim is the first one to tell the customer that such coverages should be dropped.

Tim wants to show a personal interest in the assets of his customers. He wants them to know that he treasures their treasures. And he wants them to know he is recommending to them the very same coverage he would purchase for himself if he were in their shoes.

Truly living the company's motto sometimes cost the business money in the short run. But it is also an investment. Tim knows that nine out of every ten customers he has renew with his agency, even when sometimes he is unable to beat a competitor's price.

The personal relationship he builds creates the type of loyalty that led one commercial customer to stay with Tim's firm even though his best offer was $6,000 higher than a competitor.

Tim's father and grandfather no doubt saw the business sense in building strong relationships with customers—of offering service beyond the contract. But Tim sees the spiritual sense. To him, service isn't so much an extension of the contract as it is a part of the contract—not the one his customer signed with his agency, but one Jesus signed with His blood.

Conclusion

Anyway

People are unreasonable, illogical, and self-centered,
    Love them anyway.
If you do good, people will accuse you of selfish, ulterior
motives,
    Do good anyway.
If you are successful, you win false friends and true enemies,
    Succeed anyway.
The good you do will be forgotten tomorrow,
    Do good anyway.
Honesty and frankness make you vulnerable,
    Be honest and frank anyway.
What you spent years building may be destroyed overnight,
    Build anyway.
People really need help but may attack you if you help them,
    Help people anyway.

Give the world the best you have and you will get kicked
in the teeth,

Give the world the best you've got anyway.

—From a sign on the wall of Shishu Bhavan,
the children's home in Calcutta

Where Do I Go from Here?

1. *Memorize.*

   Memorize Mark 10:43-45 and the working definition of serving mentioned in the front of this book.

2. *Audit.*

   Perform a 360-degree servanthood audit on yourself. Ask those who work over you, under you, and next to you for some feedback on their perception of your "servant performance."

3. *Pray.*

   List three people in your work environment, and begin praying every day for them. Pray for their success, growth, and advancement.

4. *Lead.*

Take fifteen minutes on serving, and lead your family through a devotional on serving others. This will help you to better personalize the servant concepts as well as educate your family towards other people.

5. *Draft.*

Write out a vision statement for your performance at work that is clearly built around your helping other people achieve, attain, and accomplish. Post it.

Notes

Chapter One

1. Edythe Draper, *Draper's Book of Quotations for the Christian World* (Wheaton, Ill.: Tyndale House Publishers, Inc., 1992), p. 555.
2. Robert K. Greenleaf, *On Becoming a Servant-Leader,* ed. Don M. Frick and Larry C. Spears (New York: Paulist Press, 1977), p. 31.

Chapter Two

1. Edythe Draper, *Draper's Book of Quotations for the Christian World* (Wheaton, Ill.: Tyndale House Publishers, Inc., 1992), p. 562.
2. Robert N. Bellah et al., *Habits of the Heart,* Perennial Library edition (New York: Harper & Row, 1985), p. vii.

Chapter Three

1. Edythe Draper, *Draper's Book of Quotations for the Christian World* (Wheaton, Ill.: Tyndale House Publishers, Inc., 1992), p. 286.

Chapter Four

1. John Blanchard, *More Gathered Gold—A Treasury of Quotations for Christmas* (Nappanee, Ind.: Evangelical Press, 1986), p. 38.

If you liked this book and would like to know more about ™Life@Work Co.™ or Cornerstone, please call us at 1-800-739-7863.

Other ways to reach us:

Mail: Post Office Box 1928
          Fayetteville, AR 72702

Fax: (501) 443-4125

E-mail: LifeWork@CornerstoneCo.com